DEPARTMENT OF THE NAVY
HEADQUARTERS UNITED STATES MARINE CORPS
3000 MARINE CORPS PENTAGON
WASHINGTON, DC 20350-3000

I0500555

ACTIVE RESERVE CAREER RECRUITER PROGRAM (ARCRP)

DEPARTMENT OF THE NAVY
HEADQUARTERS UNITED STATES MARINE CORPS
3000 MARINE CORPS PENTAGON
WASHINGTON, DC 20350-3000

IN REPLY REFER TO:
MCO 1100R.78A
MCRC
AUG 08 2007

MARINE CORPS ORDER 1100R.78A

From: Commandant of the Marine Corps
To: Distribution List

Subj: ACTIVE RESERVE CAREER RECRUITER PROGRAM (ARCRP)

Ref: (a) MCO 1001.52H
        (b) MCO P6100.12
        (c) MCO P1070.12K
        (d) MCO P1553.4A
        (e) MCO 7220.12N
        (f) MCO P1080.40C
        (g) MCO P1000.6G
        (h) MCO P1326.6D
        (i) MCO P1400.32D
        (j) MCO 1130.76A

Encl: (1) PSR 8412 Billets and Structure
        (2) Eligibility Criteria and Application Procedures for PSR
            8412 Marines
        (3) PSR 8412 PSR 8412 Billet Assignments Board Process and
            Progression
        (4) PSR 8412 Career Progression Flow Chart
        (5) PSR 8412 Application Process Timeline
        (6) PSR 8412 Formal Training Courses
        (7) PSR 8412 Timeline Billet Progression
        (8) PSR 8412 Career Progression Table
        (9) PSR 8412 Application Package

1. Situation

    a. General. The Marine Corps uses the Total Force Recruiting
concept in order to provide combatant commanders with the best
personnel this Nation can produce. The recruitment of prior service
personnel, or prior service recruiting (PSR), is reserved exclusively
for the Marine Corps Recruiting Command (MCRC), and an integral part
of this recruiting effort.

    b. Specific. The Active Reserve (AR) career recruiter (PSR 8412)
provides a body of recruiting expertise in support of the Marine Corps
total force recruiting effort. The PSR 8412 structure is contained in
enclosure (1). To highlight the importance of prior service
recruiting, the military occupational specialty (MOS) 8412 was
designated a primary MOS (PMOS) in October 1995. Since the

DISTRIBUTION STATEMENT A: Approved for public release; distribution
is unlimited.

inception of the ARCRP, the PSR 8412 has proven to be a valuable asset and has consistently demonstrated the ability to positively influence accomplishment of the recruiting mission. PSR 8412s are the backbone of MCRC's prior service recruiting force.

2. Cancellation. MCO 1100R.78.

3. Mission. This Order establishes policies and procedures for the effective management of the ARCRP in accordance with the references.

4. Execution

    a. Commander's Intent and Concept of Operations

        (1) Commander's Intent. To provide a highly skilled force of PSR 8412s to train, lead, and supervise PSR production recruiters (MOS 8411) in order to ensure consistent attainment of PSR objectives for MCRC.

        (2) Concept of Operations. The PSR 8412 force shall provide stability and continuity for PSR operations within MCRC. This will be done through the use of the tenets and principles of Systematic Recruiting and Professional Selling Skills (PSS). Maximum use of these tenets, principles, and skills will put the Marine Corps in the best posture to ensure mission accomplishment.

    b. Subordinate Element Missions

        (1) Deputy Commandant, Manpower and Reserve Affairs Department (M&RA), Reserve Affairs Division (RA)

        (a) Maintain this Order and establish the program policies and procedures, in conjunction with MCRC, necessary to effectively manage the PSR 8412 force.

        (b) Assign the PMOS 8412 to Marines who meet the requirements as set forth in enclosure (2).

        (c) Coordinate with Commanding General (CG), MCRC to assign personnel to CRC as selected by CG, MCRC per enclosure (2).

        (d) Monitor PSR 8412 personnel in the AR Program per enclosure (3).

        (e) Adjudicate MOS 8412 voidance requests for AR Marines per direction from CG, MCRC.

        (2) Commanding General, MCRC

        (a) Maintain a standing PSR 8412 Selection Board or, as required, convene a board to consider and select applicants for assignment to the CRC, and subsequent designation of primary MOS 8412

(Career Recruiter). See enclosure (2). Composition of board is at the discretion of CG, MCRC.

(b) Review applications approved by the PSR 8412 Selection Board to ensure that only qualified applicants are selected.

(c) Notify applicants of selection or non-selection.

(d) Not later than 31 January, annually, promulgate a timeline and procedures for the annual PSR 8412 Billet Assignments Board. This publication shall contain the list of potential billet vacancies as well as PSR 8412s eligible to move. See enclosure (3).

(e) Ensure completion of the PSR 8412 Billet Assignments Board not later than 3 weeks after the publication of the AR Staff Non-Commissioned Officer (SNCO) promotion board. See enclosure (3).

(f) Review and endorse PSR 8412 reassignment requests and forward to CMC (RAM) for issuance of orders for selected individuals. See enclosure (3).

(g) Manage PSR 8412 career progression per enclosures (4) through (8).

(3) Recruiting Region Commanding Generals

(a) Identify PSR 8412 requirements and initiate required table of organization changes.

(b) Review and endorse all PSR 8412 requests and forward to CG, MCRC (Attn: G-3/PSR).

(c) Provide CG, MCRC recommendations on PSR 8412 assignments per enclosure (3).

(4) District Commanding Officers (CO). Review and approve/endorse all PSR 8412 requests and forward to the regional CG (Attn: G-3/PSR).

(5) PSR Office Officers in Charge (OIC). Review and endorse all PSR 8412 requests and forward to the District CO's.

(6) PSR 8412s

(a) Inform fellow recruiters and other Marines of the ARCRP.

(b) Submit requests for assignment/reassignment as directed by MCRC (G-3/PSR).

(7) Marines requesting designation as a PSR 8412. Submit a PSR 8412 application to CG, MCRC (Attn: G-3/PSR) via the chain of

command for assignment of the 8412 MOS. Enclosure (9) provides a sample package.

       (8) <u>Director, Marine Corps Recruiting School</u>. Develop, maintain, and conduct the following PSR courses as detailed in enclosure (6):

           (a) Career Recruiter Course (CRC)

           (b) Recruiter Instructor Course

           (c) Operations Chief Course

    c. <u>Coordinating Instructions</u>. Policies and instructions governing the ARCRP are contained in the enclosures. Submit all recommendations concerning this Order or Marine Corps directives in general to CMC (ARDB) via the appropriate chain of command.

5. <u>Administration and Logistics</u>. None.

6. <u>Command and Signal</u>

    a. <u>Command</u>. This Order is applicable to the Marine Corps Total Force.

    b. <u>Signal</u>. This Order is effective the date signed.

R. S. COLEMAN
Deputy Commandant for
Manpower and Reserve Affairs

DISTRIBUTION: PCN 10200591000

PSR 8412 Billets and Structure

1. <u>PSR 8412 Billets</u>. The current authorized manning level for PSR 8412s is 40. The billets listed below are appropriate for PSR 8412s. The grades indicated are provided as guidance and suggest a career progression pattern commensurate with grade, duties, and responsibilities.

    a. <u>Prior Service Recruiting Section, MCRC (G-3)</u>

        (1) PSR Operations Chief - MGySgt (1)

        (2) MCRC NTT (PSR) - MSgt (1)

    b. <u>Prior Service Recruiting, Western Recruiting Region</u>

        (1) PSR Operations Chief - MGySgt (1)

    c. <u>Prior Service Recruiting, Eastern Recruiting Region</u>

        (1) PSR Operations Chief - MGySgt (1)

    d. <u>Prior Service Recruiting Offices</u>

        (1) Operations Chief - MGySgt or MSgt (6)

        (2) Recruiter Instructor - MSgt or GySgt (6)

        (3) Assistant Recruiter Instructor - MSgt or GySgt (2)

        (4) Area SNCOIC - MSgt or GySgt (20)

    e. <u>Marine Corps Recruiter School</u>

        (1) MGySgt (1)

        (2) GySgt (1)

Eligibility Criteria and Application Procedures for PSR 8412 Marines

1. Eligibility Criteria for Assignment of MOS 8412. The 8412 MOS shall be assigned immediately following successful completion of CRC. The following are prerequisites for AR Marines being assigned to CRC:

   a. Career designation in the AR Program.

   b. Graduate of Basic Recruiter Course (BRC) and assigned an additional MOS of 8411.

   c. Gunnery sergeants or staff sergeants who have been selected for gunnery sergeant. Master sergeants will not be considered. The ideal candidate is a gunnery sergeant with 1-3 years time in grade.

   d. Successful completion of 2 years of duty in an 8411 billet with the MCRC PSR Force. Marines who are not currently serving in an 8411 billet may be assigned to an 8411 billet for an evaluation period of up to 12 months in order to assure suitability for the 8412 MOS.

   e. Possess sufficient obligated service or agree to reenlist or extend to complete a 3-year tour as a PSR 8412. Exceptions to this 3 year obligated service requirement include only those AR Marines who reach 20 years of active service and must retire due to service or statutory grade limitations. Reference (a) applies.

   f. Prior Service Recruiting Office (PSRO) OICs will ensure that the applicant has:

      (1) The ability to positively influence the direction and quality of the recruiting effort by leading, inspiring, and motivating Marines in the recruiting environment.

      (2) Consistently achieved quantitative and qualitative recruiting mission.

      (3) Effectively adhered to and implemented recruiting policies and procedures outlined in reference (j), which is maintained by MCRC G-3, PSR Section. This document can be viewed and/or printed at https://web.mcrc.usmc.mil/ under the "Prior Service Recruiting" link.

      (4) No cases of substantiated recruiting malpractice.

      (5) No indications of unsatisfactory conduct, or financial or personal hardship.

      (6) Performed satisfactorily as a production recruiter for a minimum of 2 years and clearly demonstrated 8412 potential through documented observation.

(7) A favorable recommendation from the PSRO OIC.

(8) Been issued a Non-Commissioned Officer-in-Charge (NCOIC) assignment letter from the OIC in order to carry NCOIC duties as directed by the OIC.

g. Meet the height and weight standards and has passed a physical fitness test (PFT) within the last 6 months per reference (b). No medically excused applicants nor applicants with partial PFTs will be considered for classification as a PSR 8412.

2. Application Procedures for Classification as a PSR 8412. Submit an application requesting assignment as a PSR 8412 per enclosure (9) via the chain of command to the CG, MCRC (Attn: G-3 PSR Section). Applications will be reviewed to evaluate the applicant's qualifications and to determine if classification as a PSR 8412 is in the best interest of the Marine Corps. Applications must include:

a. An agreement to extend or reenlist for a minimum of three years of obligated service.

b. Three duty station choices that may include a request for transfer. Assignments will be made based on the needs of MCRC, the Marine Corps, and the AR program.

c. A current full-length photograph, prepared per reference (c).

d. Applicants currently serving in an 8411 billet. A Systematic Recruiting Inspection (SRI) for PSR 8412s shall be conducted at the applicant's site location by a designated Senior PSR trainer from the region, Recruiter School, or MCRC. The SRI will not be scheduled before the applicant has served a minimum of six months as a NCOIC. In addition, applicants should meet the minimum two year time in billet requirement prior to reporting to the CRC. Once all prerequisites have been met, the 8412 nominee must successfully complete the CRC course before final AA form submission to MCRC HQ.

e. Former 8411 applicants who have left recruiting and desire to return as an 8412. These applicants may be required to undergo an evaluation period performing as a NCOIC for a maximum of 12 months before being assigned the 8412 MOS. Additionally, the former PRSO must submit previous recruiting statistics and a letter of recommendation from the OIC. Upon assignment of 8412 MOS, must successfully complete first available CRC class.

PSR 8412 Billet Assignments Board Process and Progression

1. <u>General</u>. MCRC G3, PSR Section shall publish a yearly advertisement of current and expected Career Prior Service Recruiter billet vacancies, based upon retirement, permanent change of station (PCS), etc. MCRC G3, PSR Section shall conduct the PSR 8412 Billet Assignments Board following the publication of the results of the AR SNCO Selection Board. The PSR 8412 Billet Assignments Board will assign PSR 8412s to billets based upon the needs of MCRC and the Marine Corps, seniority, and previous billets held. The PSR 8412 Billet Assignments Board will present a proposed recommendation to CG, MCRC for approval. The recommendation will then be forwarded to Headquarters Marine Corps, Reserve Affairs Manpower (RAM) for orders issuance.

2. <u>PSR 8412 Assignment Board</u>. A board of at least the three members listed below shall determine the annual PSR 8412 Assignments.

    a. MCRC Sergeant Major (Board President)

    b. MCRC PSR Operations Chief

    c. MCRC G-1 8412 Monitor

3. <u>Coordinating Instructions</u>. A normal tour of duty in any PSR 8412 billet is three years. A minimum of two years time on station will normally be required before a PSR 8412 can transfer. The maximum tour of duty at any one location will normally not exceed five years. Requests for reassignment shall be made in accordance with reference (g). PSR 8412s will be assigned to billets commensurate with their grade, whenever possible. Exceptions can be made when determined to be in the best interest of MCRC and the Marine Corps.

4. <u>Development and Progression of PSR 8412s</u>

    a. <u>Concept</u>

        (1) The development and progression of PSR 8412s include opportunities to gain experience in a variety of billets and to serve in positions that are commensurate with the Marine's grade and responsibilities.

        (2) Prior Service Recruiting OICs can best influence the development and progression of PSR 8412s. They are encouraged to establish local programs to provide their PSR 8412s professional development and career progression. The program should ensure that the majority of PSR 8412s gain experience in every facet of the recruiting effort consistent with maintaining appropriate stability and continuity.

    b. <u>Promotions</u>

(1) Allocations for promotion within Occupational Field 84 will be determined based upon structure requirements. The size of the promotion zone will be set in accordance with reference (i) in order to achieve prescribed promotion opportunity guidelines.

(2) PSR 8412s may not serve in the grades of first sergeant or sergeant major.

c. <u>Professional Military Education (PME) and Specialized Skill Training for PSR 8412s</u>

(1) <u>PME</u>. Reference (d) establishes guidance for the conduct of the PME Program for all Marines. Recruiting OICs shall ensure that PSR 8412s complete of appropriate resident and nonresident courses and professional reading.

(2) <u>Specialized Skill Training for PSR 8412s</u>. Specialized skill training provides PSR 8412s with the knowledge needed to best perform their duties. Training is progressive, consisting of the formal courses outlined in enclosure (4). PSR 8412s also receive specialized skill training during seminars sponsored by the CG, MCRC. These seminars span every facet of recruiting to include salesmanship, interpersonal management, and leadership. OICs are responsible for ensuring that PSR 8412s attend specialized skill training. Upon assignment as a PSR 8412, Marines shall be scheduled to attend the next CRC.

5. <u>Special Duty Assignment (SDA) Pay for Recruiters</u>. Per references (e), (f), and (h), enlisted personnel, including ARs, who possess an MOS 8411 or 8412 and are assigned to an authorized 8411 or 8412 billet within the recruiting service, are eligible for SDA pay. SDA award level will be per the criteria in references (e), (f), and (h).

6. <u>Assignment of PSR 8412s</u>

a. <u>Obligated Service</u>. As a general rule, PSR 8412s voluntarily transferring must have three years of obligated service remaining.

b. <u>Voluntary Transfer or Reassignment</u>

(1) PSR 8412s may submit requests by AA form via the chain of command to CMC (RAM) for transfer or reassignment. All requests should contain three duty station preferences.

(2) PSR 8412s requesting transfer or reassignment involving PCS orders must have at least two years of obligated service remaining or must agree to extend or reenlist to fulfill this requirement.

(3) Transfer requests will be evaluated based on the needs of the Marine Corps, CO and OIC endorsements, and the PSR

8412's preferences. Every effort will be made to assign PSR 8412s to one of their three preferences.

    c. <u>Involuntary Transfer or Reassignment</u>. Circumstances may require either the involuntary transfer or reassignment of PSR 8412s due to the needs of the Marine Corps. In these cases, CMC (RAM) may direct transfer or reassignment without regard for length of tour or obligated service. Such transfers or reassignments will not be directed routinely.

7. <u>Involuntary Voidance of the 8412 MOS</u>. When circumstances merit involuntary voidance of the 8412 MOS, OIC's should recommend relief for cause or for the good of the service. Submit recommendations per reference (h) and the Prior Service Recruiting Guidebook to the CG, MCRC. If relief is approved, the CG, MCRC will notify CMC (RAM) and request voidance of the 8412 MOS. PSR 8412s who are relieved for cause are subject to administrative action normally taken in any involuntary relief or voidance case per reference (i).

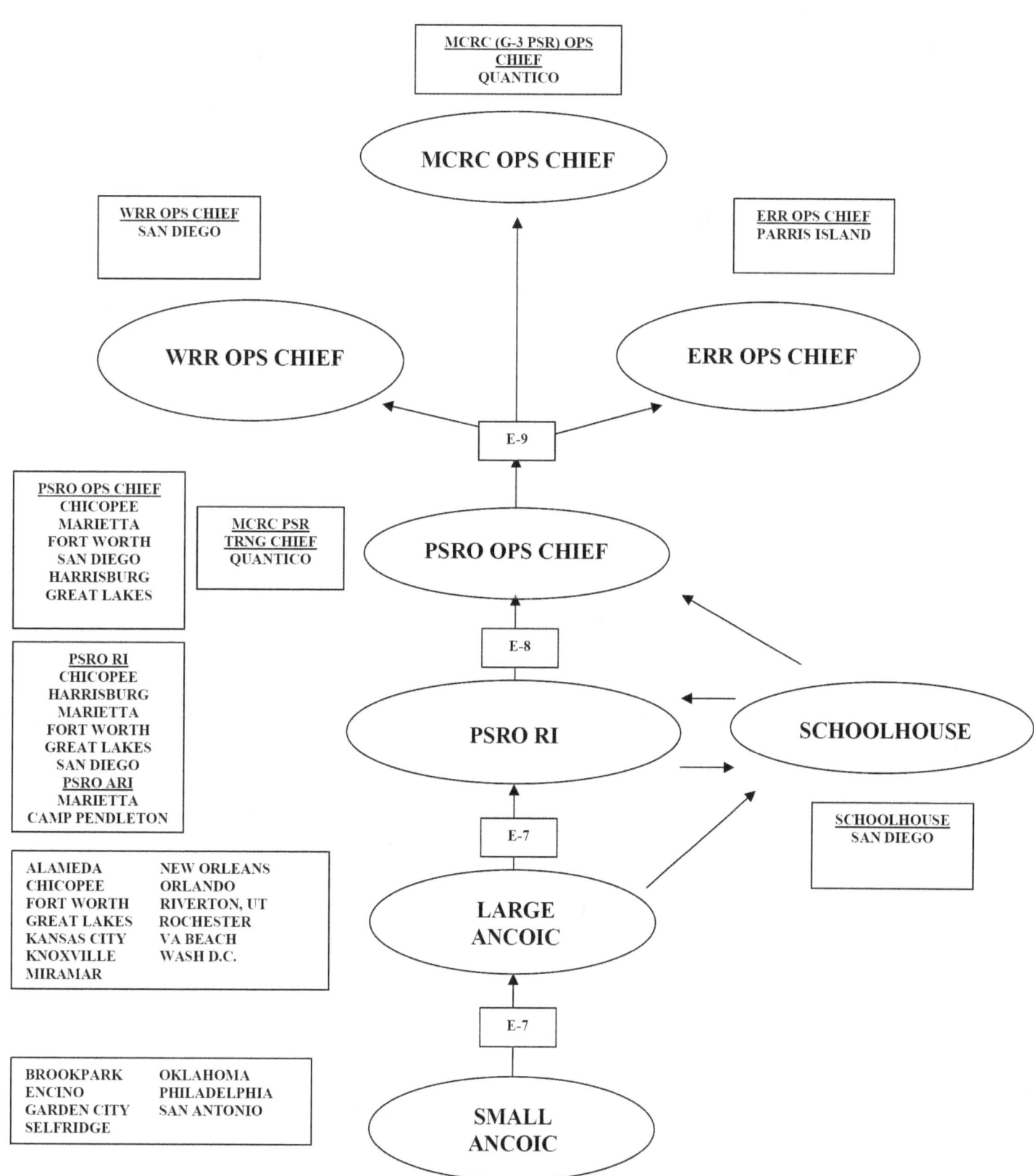

Figure 1-1.--PSR 8412 Career Progression Flow Chart

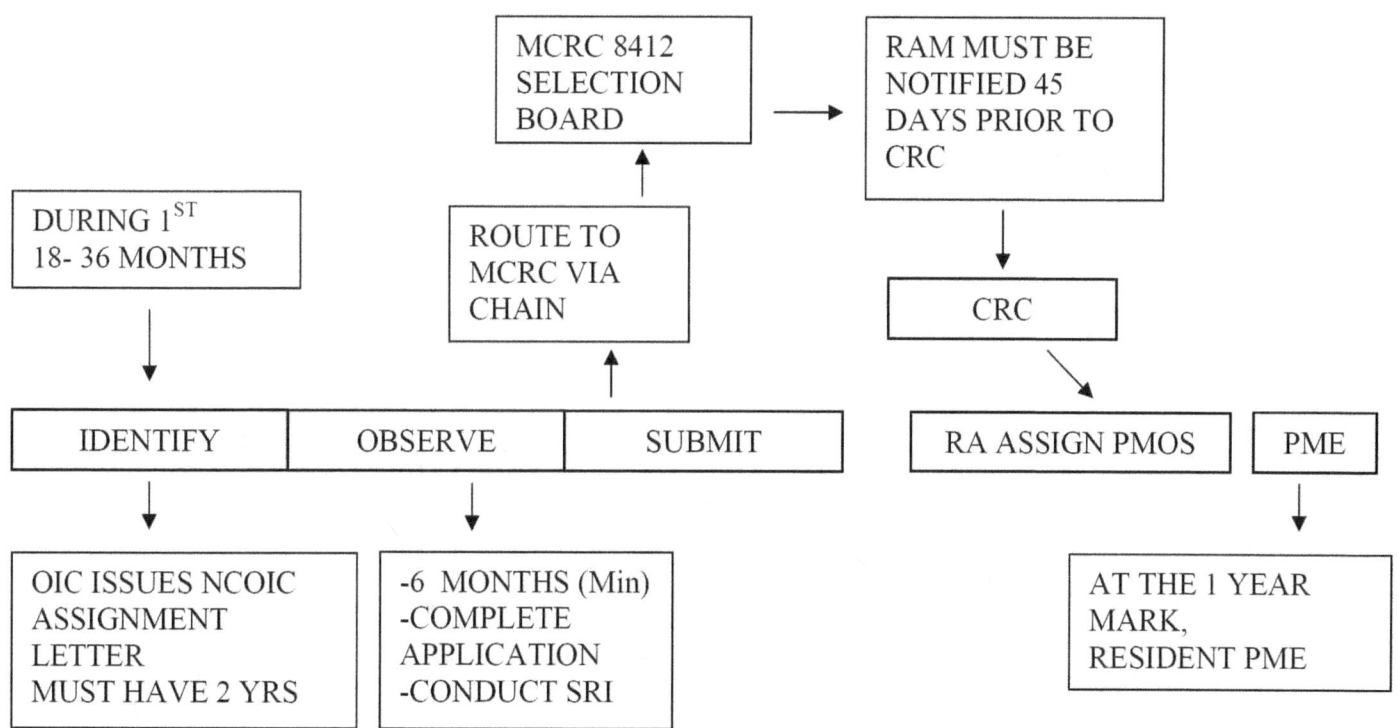

Figure 2-1.--PSR 8412 Application Process Timeline

PSR 8412 Formal Training Courses

1. <u>Career Recruiter Course (CRC)</u>. The CRC is designed to provide all newly selected PSR 8412 candidates with advanced sales, coaching, training, and management skills. The course emphasizes the development of skills necessary to lead, evaluate, train, and coach the sales force.

2. <u>Recruiter Instructor Course (RIC)</u>. The RIC is designed to provide knowledge to new Recruiter Instructors about problem solving, command group functioning, and time management. A key component of the course emphasizes "Tools for Training Excellence" presented by a certified Marine Corps Trainer. This seminar is designed to provide Recruiter Instructors with the skills needed to develop, present, and teach courses and other instruction.

3. <u>Operations Chief Course</u>. This course is three days long and focuses on management and Automated Systematic Recruiting. All newly selected Operations Chiefs should attend the first available course.

PSR 8412 Timeline Billet Progression

1. Gunnery Sergeants - 20

    - PSR Area SNCOICs
        - Chicopee, MA
        - Philadelphia, PA
        - Rochester, NY
        - Garden City, NY
        - Washington, D.C.
        - Virginia Beach, VA
        - Brookpark, OH
        - Alameda, CA
        - Miramar, CA
        - Riverton, UT
        - Fort Worth, TX
        - Oklahoma City, OK
        - San Antonio, TX
        - Kansas City, MO
        - Selfridge, MI
        - Great Lakes, IL
        - Encino, CA
        - New Orleans, LA
        - Orlando, FL
        - Knoxville, TN

2. Senior Gunnery Sergeants - 5

    - PSR Recruiter Instructors (RIs)
        - Chicopee, MA
        - Great Lakes, IL
        - Marietta, GA (ARI)
        - Camp Pendleton, CA (ARI)

    - PSR Schoolhouse
        - San Diego, CA

3. Master Sergeants - 11

    - PSR Operations Chiefs
        - Chicopee, MA
        - New Cumberland, PA
        - Marietta, GA
        - Fort Worth, TX
        - Great Lakes, IL

    - PSR Recruiter Instructors (RIs)
        - New Cumberland, PA
        - Marietta, GA
        - Fort Worth, TX
        - Camp Pendleton, CA
        - Quantico, VA (PSR trainer/NTT rep)

    - PSR Schoolhouse
        - San Diego, CA

4. Master Gunnery Sergeants - 4

    - Quantico, VA (MCRC Operations Chief)
    - San Diego, CA (WRR Operations Chief)
    - Parris Island, SC (ERR Operations Chief)
    - Camp Pendleton, CA (PSRO-12 Operations Chief)

Requirement	GySgt	MSgt	MGySgt
USMC PME	• Warfighting • Advanced Course Resident • Advanced Course Nonresident	• GySgt Requirements • E8 Seminar	• GySgt / MSgt Requirements • PME Development
8412 ASSIGNMENT	• ANCOIC • RI • ARI • MCRC QC CHIEF	• OPS Chiefs • RI • Schoolhouse • MCRC PSR TRNG CHIEF	• MCRC OPS • ERR/WRR OPS • District OPS Chief
PSS SKILLS/SPECIAL SKILLS	TFCE T3 APPLICATIONS T3	TFCE T3 APPLICATIONS T3 * TFTE * FSIC * CDC Master Trainer	
RECRUITING EXPERIENCE	2-5 yrs	5-10 yrs	10+
RETENTION POINT/TIME IN SERVICE	22 yrs	26 yrs	30 yrs
TIME IN ASSIGNED BILLETS	2-3 yrs	2-3 yrs	2-3 yrs

Figure 3-1.--PSR 8412 Career Progression Table

PSR 8412 Application Package

PSR 8412 CHECKLIST (See examples below)

1. Applicant's Request letter
2. AA Form
3. First Endorsement PSR OIC (Include Stats chart)
4. Second Endorsement District CO
5. Third Endorsement Region CG
6. Fourth Endorsement MCRC CG
7. Official digital photo (Service "C" Uniform, Ribbons, without cover)
8. CRC certificate
9. PSR OIC NCOIC Appointment letter
10. Systematic Recruiting Inspection (SRI) Checklist

FOR FORMER PSR/TR 8411 REQUESTING TO RETURN

1. Applicant's Request letter
2. AA Form
3. Endorsement from current CO
4. Letter of recommendation from former PSR OIC. Stats if available from prior recruiting tour
5. Official digital photo (Service "C" Uniform, Ribbons, without cover)
6. Upon assignment of 8412 MOS, must successfully complete first available CRC class.

Command Letterhead
Address

1221
Originator
Date

From: Applicant (Grade, Name, SSN, MOS/Component)
To: Commandant of the Marine Corps (RAM-2)
Via: (1) Officer In Charge, Prior Service Recruiting Office __
       (2) Commanding Officer, _____ Marine Corps District
       (3) Commanding General, _____ Recruiting Region
       (4) Commanding General, Marine Corps Recruiting Command

Subj: APPLICATION FOR ASSIGNMENT AS ACTIVE RESERVE CAREER
       RECRUITER

Ref: (a) MCO 1100R.78A

Encl: (1) NAVMC 10274, Administrative Action Form requesting
           extension of recruiting tour (If required)
       (2) Photograph
       (3) PSR OIC NCOIC Appointment letter
       (4) Systematic Recruiting Inspection (SRI) if applicable
       (5) CRC certificate

1. I am applying for assignment as a Career Recruiter (PMOS
8412). Per the reference, the enclosures are submitted in
support of my request.

2. Appropriate remarks as required.

                              I. M. MARINE

           Figure 4-1.--Format of an Applicant Request Letter

Command Letterhead
Address

1221
Originator
Date

From: Applicant (Grade, Name, SSN, MOS/Component)
To: Commandant of the Marine Corps (RAM-2)
Via: (1) Commanding Officer _____
       (2) Commanding General, Marine Corps Recruiting Command

Subj: APPLICATION FOR ASSIGNMENT AS ACTIVE RESERVE CAREER
       RECRUITER FROM FORMER 8411

Ref: (a) MCO 1100R.78

Encl: (1) NAVMC 10274, Administrative Action Form requesting
           extension of recruiting tour (If required)
       (2) PSR OIC LOR (w/stats)
       (3) Photograph

1. I am applying for assignment as a Career Recruiter (PMOS
8412). Enclosure (1) is provided per reference (a). Enclosure
(2) is submitted in support of my request. Enclosure (3) has
been prepared in according with reference (a).

2. Appropriate remarks as required.

                              I. M. MARINE

Figure 5-1.--Format of an Applicant Request Letter from former 8411

ADMINISTRATIVE ACTION (5216)

NAVMC 10274 (REV. 3-93) (EF)
Previous editions will be used
SN: 0109-LF-063-3200 U/I: PADS OF 100

1. ACTION NO.	2. SSIC/FILE NO.
	1100
3. DATE	

4. FROM (Grade, Name, SSN, MOS, or CO, Pers. O., etc.)
Staff Sergeant Im A. Marine 123 45 6789/0193

5. ORGANIZATION AND STATION (Complete address)
(Unit title and address)

6. VIA (As required)
(1) Chain of Command
(2) Commanding General, WRR or ERR

7.

TO:
Commanding General, MCRC
Headquarters, U. S. Marine Corps
3280 Russell Road
Quantico, VA 22134-5103

8. NATURE OF ACTION/SUBJECT
REQUEST FOR ASSIGNMENT AS A PRIOR
SERVICE CAREER RECRUITER (MOS 8412)

9. COPY TO (As required)

10. REFERENCE OR AUTHORITY (if applicable)
(a) MCO 1100R.78

11. ENCLOSURES (if any)
(1) Current photograph

12. SUPPLEMENTAL INFORMATION (Reduce to minimum wording - type name of orginator and sign 3 lines below text)

1. Per the reference, I am eligible for and am applying for the Active Reserve Career Recruiter Program. If approved, I agree to extend or reenlist to complete a minimum of 3 years.

2. The following information is provided:
    a. Date designated as "Career" on AR Program:
    b. AFADBD:
    c. PEBD:
    d. DOR:
    e. Date current recruiting tour began:
    f. Previous recruiting tours:
    g. Recruiting Awards:
    h. Date last PFT: Score:

3. If relieved of duties as a Career Recruiter and subsequently have my 8412 MOS vioded, I understand that I could be assigned to one of my additional MOS's, be released from active duty.

I. M. MARINE

13. PROCESSING ACTION. (Complete processing action in item 12 or on reverse. Endorse by rubber stamp where practicable.)

Designed using FormFlow 2.15, HQMC/ARAE May 98

Figure 6-1.--Format of an Applicant AA Form

Command Letterhead
Address

1221
Originator
Date

FIRST ENDORSEMENT on

From: Officer in Charge, Prior Service Recruiting Office ___
To: Commandant of the Marine Corps (RAM-2)
Via: (1) Commanding Officer, _____ Marine Corps District
        (2) Commanding General, _____ Recruiting Region
        (3) Commanding General, Marine Corps Recruiting Command

Subj: APPLICATION FOR ASSIGNMENT ACTIVE RESERVE (AR) CAREER
        RECRUITER

Ref: (a) MCO 1100R.78A

Encl: (1) as required

1. The information contained in the basic application has
been verified and is correct. The applicant does/does not meet
the basic requirements and is/is not fully qualified for the
Active Reserve Career Recruiter Program (PMOS 8412) per the
reference. I do/do not recommend this Marine for selection as a
Career Recruiter. (If not qualified and recommended, explain in
the paragraph 5.) Enclosure (_) is submitted in support of this
request.

2. Performance as a recruiter/NCOIC (tour-to-date).

PERFORMANCE AS A RECRUITER/NCOIC (tour-to-date)	
Production Recruiter	Area NCOIC
PSR Site:	PSR Sites:
Dates: From: To:	Dates: From: To:
Production Months:	# of Sites Supervise:
Net Production Average:	# of Production Recruiter Supervised:
SMCR Officer: /	Net Production Average for AOR:
SMCR Enlisted: /	Accession Quality Package Grade for AOR:
IMA Officer: /	8412 Course Completed:
IMA Enlisted: /	SMCR Off / SMCR Enl
* SMCR Attrition %	IMA Off / IMA Enl
Accession Quality Package Average:	* Attrition for AOR:
Recruiter Courses Completed:	# Of Investigation/Inquires:
Recruiter Disciplinary Actions:	# Recruiters Relieved while ANCOIC
	RFC: GOS:

Figure 7-1.--Format of an Applicant First Endorsement

Subj: APPLICATION FOR ASSIGNMENT ACTIVE RESERVE (AR) CAREER
RECRUITER

3. OIC's Remarks. These remarks will address the Marine's
ability to lead, train and supervise Marines in a recruiting
environment, including a brief explanation on any
investigations/inquiries and/or recruiter relief. (Attach
additional pages if necessary).

I. M. MARINE

Figure 7-2.--Format of an Applicant First Endorsement--Continued

Command Letterhead
Address

1221
Originator
Date

SECOND ENDORSEMENT on

From: Commanding Officer, _____ Marine Corps District
To: Commandant of the Marine Corps (RAM-2)
Via: (1) Commanding General, _____ Recruiting Region
       (2) Commanding General, Marine Corps Recruiting Command

Subj: APPLICATION FOR ASSIGNMENT AS ACTIVE RESERVE (AR) CAREER
       RECRUITER

Ref: (a) MCO 1100R.78A

Encl: (1) as required

1. Forwarded, recommending approval.

2. Narrative summary that addresses the Marine's ability to lead
and supervise Marines in a recruiting environment. Comments
should also address significant issues, which may have surfaced
during the completion of the PSR 8412 Checklist.

3. Per the reference, enclosures (_) and (_) are provided.

                        I. M. MARINE

        Figure 8-1.--Format of an Applicant Second Endorsement

Command Letterhead
Address

1221
Originator
Date

THIRD ENDORSEMENT on

From: Commanding General, _____ Recruiting Region
To: Commandant of the Marine Corps (RAM-2)
Via: Commanding General, Marine Corps Recruiting Command

Subj: APPLICATION FOR ASSIGNMENT AS AN ACTIVE RESERVE (AR)
       CAREER RECRUITER

Ref: (a) MCO 1100R.78A

1. Per the reference, forwarded, recommending approval.

2. Appropriate remarks as required.

                              I. M. MARINE

Figure 9-1.--Format of an Applicant Third Endorsement

Command Letterhead
Address

1221
Originator
Date

FOURTH ENDORSEMENT on

From: Commanding General, Marine Corps Recruiting Command
To: Commandant of the Marine Corps (RAM-2)

Subj: APPLICATION FOR ASSIGNMENT AS AN ACTIVE RESERVE (AR)
       CAREER RECRUITER

Ref: (a) MCO 1100R.78A

1. Per the reference, forwarded, recommending
approval/disapproval and assignment of PMOS of 8412 effective
date of completion of Career Recruiter Course.

2. Appropriate remarks as required.

                         I. M. MARINE

Figure 10-1.--Format of an Applicant Fourth Endorsement

OFFICIAL PHOTO

Note: Ensure Photo contains:

Last Name
First Name
Middle Initial(s)
Rank
PMOS
SSN
Height
Weight
Body Fat % if applicable
Date (YYMMDD)

Figure 11-1.--Example Applicant Photograph

www.ingramcontent.com/pod-product-compliance
Lightning Source LLC
Chambersburg PA
CBHW080735290526
45790CB00008B/3207